FEDERAL ELECTRICITY SUBSIDIES

FEDERAL ELECTRICITY SUBSIDIES

GOVERNMENT ACCOUNTABILITY OFFICE

Nova Science Publishers, Inc.

New York

NOTICE TO THE READER
The Publisher has taken reasonable care in the preparation of this book, but makes no expressed or implied warranty of any kind and assumes no responsibility for any errors or omissions. No liability is assumed for incidental or consequential damages in connection with or arising out of information contained in this book. The Publisher shall not be liable for any special, consequential, or exemplary damages resulting, in whole or in part, from the readers' use of, or reliance upon, this material.

Independent verification should be sought for any data, advice or recommendations contained in this book. In addition, no responsibility is assumed by the publisher for any injury and/or damage to persons or property arising from any methods, products, instructions, ideas or otherwise contained in this publication.

This publication is designed to provide accurate and authoritative information with regard to the subject matter covered herein. It is sold with the clear understanding that the Publisher is not engaged in rendering legal or any other professional services. If legal or any other expert assistance is required, the services of a competent person should be sought. FROM A DECLARATION OF PARTICIPANTS JOINTLY ADOPTED BY A COMMITTEE OF THE AMERICAN BAR ASSOCIATION AND A COMMITTEE OF PUBLISHERS.

LIBRARY OF CONGRESS CATALOGING-IN-PUBLICATION DATA

Federal electricity subsidies / G.A.O. (author).
   p. cm.
"This book is an excerpted, indexed edition of GAO report GAO 08-102, dated October 2007."
ISBN 978-1-60456-769-4 (softcover)
1.   Electric utilities--Subsidies--United States. 2.   United States. Dept. of Energy--Appropriations and expenditures. 3.   Federal aid to energy development--United States.   I. United States. Government Accountability Office.
   HD9685.U5F416 2008
   354.4'92730973--dc22
                200802318

Published by Nova Science Publishers, Inc. ✢ New York

CONTENTS

PREFACE

October 26, 2007

The Honorable Thomas Carper
Chairman
Subcommittee on Clean Air and Nuclear Safety
Committee on Environment and Public Works
United States Senate

The Honorable Lamar Alexander
Ranking Member
Subcommittee on Public Sector Solutions to Global Warming, Oversight,
and Children's Health Protection
Committee on Environment and Public Works
United States Senate

Electricity is vital to our daily lives, powering homes, businesses, and industries. Presently, electricity is generated largely by coal and other fossil fuels and nuclear power, with hydropower, and, to a lesser extent, renewable energy sources, such as wind. Because of electricity's importance to producers, consumers, and businesses, the federal government has undertaken a wide range of programs to develop the electricity sector, which includes fuel suppliers, electric utilities, and others in the electricity industry. These programs have sought to, among other things, develop the nation's electrical infrastructure, influence the types of fuels used to produce electricity, increase the use of renewable energy, and limit the harmful effects of electricity production.

These programs are financed through federal subsidies, broadly defined as payments made or benefits provided by the federal government to encourage certain desired activities or behaviors. For example, the federal government has, for many years, funded research and development (R&D) on fossil fuels, nuclear energy, renewable energy, other energy technologies, and related efforts through the Department of Energy (DOE). In addition, the federal government has provided favorable tax treatment, such as tax credits to companies that make certain types of energy investments. These tax preferences—which are legally known as tax expenditures—result in forgone revenue for the federal government. The revenue losses can be viewed as spending channeled through the tax system.

As requested, we are providing information on (1) federal funding DOE receives for electricity-related R&D, including funding by type of fuel; (2) tax expenditures the federal government provides to subsidize electricity production, including expenditures by type of fuel; and (3) other ways the federal government subsidizes electricity. As discussed with your offices, we examined federal electricity-related subsidies over a 6-year period, from fiscal year 2002 through fiscal year 2007.

ABBREVIATIONS

BPA	Bonneville Power Administration
CBO	Congressional Budget Office
CREBs	Clean Renewable Energy Bonds
CRS	Congressional Research Service
DOE	Department of Energy
EIA	Energy Information Administration
FERC	Federal Energy Regulatory Commission
NRC	Nuclear Regulatory Commission
OMB	Office of Management and Budget
PMA	power marketing administration
R&D	research and development
RUS	Rural Utilities Service
SEPA	Southeastern Power Administration
SWPA	Southwestern Power Administration
Treasury	Department of the Treasury
TVA	Tennessee Valley Authority
USDA	Department of Agriculture
WAPA	Western Area Power Administration

Chapter 1

RESULTS IN BRIEF[*]

We estimate that DOE's appropriations for electricity-related R&D, adjusted for inflation, totaled $11.5 billion from fiscal year 2002 through fiscal year 2007.[1] These appropriations grew by 35 percent during the 6-year period we examined, increasing from $1.6 billion in fiscal year 2002 to $2.2 billion in fiscal year 2007. Funding for DOE's electricity-related R&D by fuel type (nuclear, fossil fuel, and renewables) include the following programs:

- *Nuclear programs.* Nuclear programs received the largest share of electricity-related R&D funding, with appropriations totaling $6.2 billion from fiscal year 2002 through fiscal year 2007. Appropriations for nuclear programs grew by 59 percent, increasing from $775 million in fiscal year 2002 to $1.2 billion in fiscal year 2007. The greatest variation in funding within these programs occurred in the environmental cleanup program, which funds the cleanup of sites contaminated by nuclear research. Funding for this program increased from $168 million in fiscal year 2002 to $462 million in fiscal year 2005, before declining to $350 million in fiscal year 2007. Other nuclear energy programs include research on fusion energy and the Advanced Fuel Cycle Initiative, which seeks to reduce nuclear fuel waste requiring geologic disposal.

---

[*] Excerpted from GAO Report GAO 08-102, dated October 2007.

- *Fossil fuel programs.* Fossil fuel programs were appropriated $3.1 billion in electricity-related R&D funding from fiscal year 2002 through fiscal year 2007. Appropriations for these programs were relatively constant during the 6-year period we examined. Appropriations totaled $531 million in fiscal year 2002, peaked at $574 million in fiscal year 2004, and then returned to $531 million in fiscal year 2007. Most of the funding variation within these programs was due to the Clean Coal Power Initiative, which is aimed at accelerating the deployment of advanced technologies to reduce air emissions and other pollutants from coal-burning power plants. Funding for the Clean Coal Power Initiative decreased from $210 million in fiscal year 2004 to $62 million in fiscal year 2005, before increasing to $75 million in fiscal year 2007. Other significant fossil fuel energy programs include the fuels and power systems program, which provides research funding aimed at reducing coal-burning power plant carbon emissions, and the FutureGen program, which focuses on the technical capability of coproducing electricity and hydrogen with near-zero emissions.

- *Renewable programs.* Renewable programs were appropriated $1.4 billion in electricity-related R&D funding from fiscal year 2002 through fiscal year 2007. During this period, appropriations for these programs grew by 23 percent, increasing from $248 million in fiscal year 2002 to $305 million in fiscal year 2007. Variations in funding were primarily attributable to funding for the Solar program, which makes up the largest share of renewable program funding. Here, funding more than doubled between fiscal year 2006 and 2007, rising from $99 million to $203 million. Other renewable energy programs include wind, biomass, and geothermal programs. The hydrogen R&D program was not included in our analysis as hydrogen primarily is used as an alternative fuel for transportation. Based on our review of the Department of the Treasury (Treasury) estimates, the sum of revenue loss estimates associated with tax expenditures specifically related to electricity totaled $18.2 billion from fiscal year 2002 to fiscal year 2007.[2] Over this period, revenue loss estimates associated with these tax expenditures increased by 88 percent, growing from $2.2 billion to $4.1 billion annually. Electricity-related tax expenditures by type of fuel include the following:

- *Fossil fuels.* Fossil fuels received the largest share of electricity-related tax expenditures. We estimate that tax expenditures to support electricity production from fossil fuels totaled $13.7 billion from fiscal year 2002 through fiscal year 2007. Revenue loss estimates associated with these tax expenditures grew by 43 percent during the 6-year period we reviewed, increasing from $1.9 billion in fiscal year 2002 to $2.7 billion in fiscal year 2007. These revenue loss estimates stemmed from 12 different tax expenditures. The largest tax expenditure supporting electricity production from fossil fuels was the alternative fuel production credit, which Treasury estimated at $2.1 billion for fiscal year 2007.[3]

- *Renewables.* We estimate that tax expenditures to support electricity production from renewable sources totaled $2.8 billion from fiscal year 2002 through fiscal year 2007. Revenue loss estimates associated with these tax expenditures grew by 232 percent during the 6-year period we reviewed, increasing from $238 million in fiscal year 2002 to $790 million in fiscal year 2007. These revenue loss estimates stemmed from three tax expenditures—Clean Renewable Energy Bond tax credits, exclusion of interest on energy facility bonds, and the new technology tax credit for renewable electricity production and renewable energy investment. The new technology credit, which reduces the cost of electricity generation from wind, geothermal, and solar energy, is the largest tax expenditure directed at renewable electricity production. Revenue loss estimates for this tax credit totaled $690 million in fiscal year 2007.

- *Nuclear.* We did not identify tax expenditures directed at nuclear power production during the 6-year period we examined. A key tax expenditure directed at nuclear power production, the advanced nuclear power facilities production tax credit, was enacted in the 2005 Energy Policy Act. However, this tax credit has not been used because no nuclear power plant has been built recently. As requested, we also identified a number of other potential federal government subsidies of electricity production. However, as discussed with your staff during our briefing, additional work would be required in order to determine the extent to which these activities are subsidies and to develop reasonable estimates. Among these:

- The federal government provides low-cost financing to federal power entities. For example, the power marketing administrations (PMA)[4] other than the Bonneville Power Administration (BPA) finance capital expenditures through federally appropriated debt. While PMAs repay appropriated debt to Treasury with interest, financing subsidies may exist if Treasury's cost of funds is greater than the interest rates on PMA-appropriated debt. Critics also have noted the rates, terms, and conditions of PMA debt may be preferential when compared to market rates, terms, and conditions.

- The Department of Agriculture's (USDA) Rural Utilities Service[5] provides loans and loan guarantees to rural electric cooperatives at low rates. Authorized amounts of these electricity loans and loan guarantees totaled $21.9 billion from fiscal year 2002 to fiscal year 2006.

- The federal government, through the Price-Anderson Act, limits nuclear plant operator liability for accidents. This may be considered a subsidy because it could reduce insurance coverage needs and related insurance costs for nuclear plant operators.

Chapter 2

SCOPE AND METHODOLOGY

To estimate the federal funding DOE has received for electricity-related R&D, we conducted detailed reviews of DOE's R&D budget documents and included prior year balances and transfers from other agencies in our analysis, as well as funding for nuclear fusion energy, considered basic research by some. We also used Energy Information Administration (EIA) data on the types, amounts, and percentage of fuels used to produce electricity to estimate DOE's electricity-related R&D spending by fuel type. We discussed our allocation methodology with EIA officials.

To estimate the amount of tax expenditures the federal government provides to subsidize electricity production, we reviewed Treasury's tax expenditure data and identified specific electricity-related tax expenditures. We excluded broad tax expenditures available to most businesses. We used Treasury revenue loss estimates to determine the costs of these tax expenditures from fiscal year 2002 through fiscal year 2007. We also used EIA data on the types, amounts and percentage of fuels used to produce electricity to assign the electricity-related portion of these tax expenditure estimates by fuel type. We also reviewed our allocation methodology with EIA officials and staff in Treasury's Office of Tax Analysis.

To identify other ways the federal government subsidizes electricity, we reviewed relevant reports and studies prepared by GAO and other federal agencies including the Congressional Budget Office, the Congressional Research Service, and EIA. We reviewed studies by trade associations and nongovernmental groups. We interviewed relevant federal agency staff and other experts at trade associations and non-governmental groups. We conducted limited reviews of activities at the PMAs, the Tennessee Valley

Authority, and USDA. In addition, we identified measures to calculate net federal financing support for loan and loan guarantee programs.

Several limitations apply to our review, including:

- We did not analyze subsidies related to electricity end use or consumption, such as those designed to promote energy efficiency and conservation or to provide low-income energy assistance.
- We did not gather data on possible electricity-related R&D funding by federal agencies other than DOE.
- We did not audit or verify data provided by agencies. We determined that DOE budget data were sufficiently reliable to provide useful information about the agency's electricity-related R&D funding.
- Although we present the tax expenditure estimates in aggregate and the sums are reliable as a gauge of general magnitude, they do not take into account interactions between individual provisions. We determined that Treasury's list of tax expenditures and revenue loss estimates were sufficiently reliable to provide perspective on electricity-related tax programs.
- We did not attempt to determine the market value of electricity-related subsidies.

We conducted this performance audit from April 2007 through September 2007 in accordance with generally accepted government auditing standards. Those standards require that we plan and perform the audit to obtain sufficient, appropriate evidence to provide a reasonable basis for our findings and conclusions based on our audit objectives. We believe that the evidence obtained provides a reasonable basis for our findings and conclusions based on our audit objectives.

APPENDIX I: BRIEFING TO THE SENATE COMMITTEE ON ENVIRONMENT AND PUBLIC WORKS

FEDERAL ELECTRICITY SUBSIDIES BRIEFING TO THE SENATE COMMITTEE ON ENVIRONMENT AND PUBLIC WORKS SEPTEMBER 6, 2007

Background

Subsidies Represent the Provision of Benefits to a Group

Subsidies are broadly defined as payments or benefits provided to encourage certain desired activities or behaviors.

In budget terms, subsidies are a payment or benefit made by the federal government where the benefit exceeds the cost to the beneficiary. Types of subsidies can include:

- Preferential provisions in the tax code (e.g., tax credits, deductions, special tax rates, or deferrals) referred to as tax expenditures.
- Provision of loans, goods, and services to the public at prices lower than market value. These include interest subsidies.[1]

---

[1] GAO, A Glossary of Terms Used in the Federal Budget Process, GAO-05-734SP (Washington, D.C.: Sept. 2005).

Subsidies are often provided to implement federal policy, such as to encourage development or use of specific technologies.

In some cases, such as research and development (R&D), subsidies may be provided well in advance of desired activities or behaviors.

Table 1. Electricity Subsidies May Not Be Fuel Specific

Phase	Examples of federal subsidies
Fuel exploration and extraction	•Tax treatment of geological and geophysical expenditures. •Capital gains treatment of royalties on coal.
Power generation	•Tax credits for renewable electricity production. •Department of Energy (DOE) R&D funding on advanced generation technologies.
Power transmission and distribution	•USDA Rural Development loans and loan guarantees for capital expenses.
End use	•Tax credits for the purchase of energy efficient appliances. •DOE Weatherization Assistance Program.
Environmental, health, and safety	•Partial expensing for advanced mine safety equipment. •Liability limits for nuclear power plant accidents.

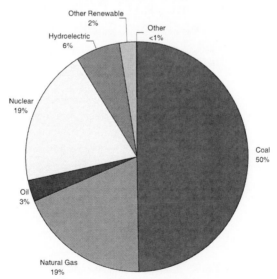

Source: GAO analysis of data provided by the Energy Information Administration.

Note: Total individual slices may not total 100% due to individual rounding.

Figure 1. 2005 Generation Mix Dominated by Fossil Fuels and Nuclear

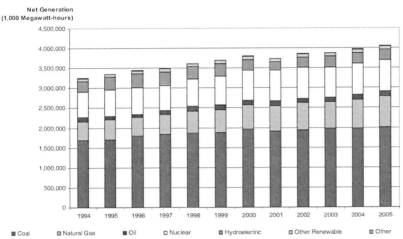

Source: GAO analysis of data provided by Energy Information Administration.

Figure 2. Electricity Generation Continues to Rise

Objectives

1. How much federal funding has DOE received for electricity-related R&D, including funding by type of fuel?
2. How much does the federal government provide in the form of tax expenditures to subsidize electricity, including tax expenditures by type of fuel?
3. In what other ways does the federal government subsidize electricity?

Scope and Methodology

Reviewed relevant reports and studies

- Prior GAO reports
- Federal agency reports (CBO, CRS, EIA)
- Studies by trade associations and nongovernmental groups

Interviewed key experts

- Federal agency staff (EIA, CBO, CRS, BPA, Treasury, TVA, USDA, NRC)
- Experts at key trade associations and nongovernmental groups

Conducted detailed reviews of

- DOE R&D budgets
- Treasury tax expenditure data

Developed estimates of how much of the subsidies were electricity-related based on EIA data. Conducted limited reviews of activities at PMAs, TVA, and USDA. Identified measures to calculate net federal financing support for:

- Loan and loan guarantee programs and federal power programs
- Subsidies stemming from programs and laws related to nuclear power

Consulted with EIA on related ongoing work (expected November 2007).

All amounts reported are adjusted for inflation utilizing 2007 as the base year.

Our work was completed from April 2007 through September 2007 according to generally accepted government auditing standards.

Limitations

We analyzed federal electricity subsidies from fiscal year 2002 to fiscal year 2007, and our analysis does not include subsidies before fiscal year 2002 or projected to occur after fiscal year 2007.

We did not analyze subsidies related to electricity end use or consumption such as energy efficiency, conservation, and low-income energy assistance in the scope of our work.

Due to limited time frame, we did not gather data on possible electricity-related R&D funding by federal agencies other than DOE.

- Department of Defense, the National Aeronautics and Space Administration, and the Department of Commerce

Our R&D funding analysis included prior year balances and transfers from other agencies noted in DOE appropriation documents. We also included DOE R&D funding for fusion energy, considered basic research by some, under nuclear power. Where data were available, we analyzed federal electricity subsidies based on the cost to the federal government to provide them. We did not attempt to determine the market value of subsidies. We did not audit or verify data provided by the agencies. We determined that DOE budget data were sufficiently reliable to provide useful information about the agency's electricity-related R&D funding.

Although we present tax expenditure estimates in the aggregate and the sums are reliable as a gauge of general magnitude, they do not take into account interactions between individual provisions. As a rule, we excluded broad tax expenditures available to most businesses.

We did not evaluate whether subsidies occur in federal policies such as the royalty treatment of resource extraction on federal land, charges for the use of federally-owned resources (such as land that is used for hydropower generation), and differential treatment of electric power generation plants with respect to pollution control. We also did not review possible subsidies related to trust fund liabilities of several funds, such as the Abandoned Mine Reclamation Fund and the Black Lung Liability Fund. (See GAO, *Renewable Energy: Wind Power's Contribution to Electric Power Generation and Impact on Farms and Communities*, GAO-04-756 (Washington, D.C.: Sept. 3, 2004) for a fuller discussion of the potential hidden subsidies stemming from environmental and health costs.)

Results in Brief

For electricity-related R&D, we estimate

- DOE received $11.5 billion (2007 dollars) in funding from FY2002 to FY2007.
- Funding grew by 35 percent from FY2002 to FY2007.
- Funding spread across several fuels: about $6.2 billion was provided to nuclear, $3.1 billion to fossil fuels, and $1.4 billion to renewables.

For electricity-related tax expenditures, we estimate

- Tax expenditures totaled $18.2 billion (2007 dollars) from FY2002 to FY2007.
- Grew by 88 percent from FY2002 to FY2007.
- Tax expenditures largely go to fossil fuels: about $13.7 billion was provided to fossil fuels and $2.8 billion to renewables.
- We did not include the credit for production from advanced nuclear power facilities because there is no current revenue loss from the credit as advanced nuclear facilities have yet to be constructed.

Federal loan and loan guarantees, preferred borrowing, and other activities may also subsidize electricity.

Research and Development

DOE Electricity-Related R&D Funding Totals $11.5 Billion (2007 dollars) from FY2002 to FY2007 and Increased by About 35% over this Period

We estimate that DOE electricity-related R&D funding totaled $11.5 billion from FY2002 to FY2007.

- Nuclear: $6.2 billion
- Fossil Fuels: $3.1 billion
- Renewables: $1.4 billion
- Transmission: $0.7 billion

(Amounts for nuclear, fossil fuels, renewables and transmission do not add up to $11.5 billion due to rounding.)

R&D funding across all fuel types increased by 35% from FY2002 through FY2007, from $1.6 billion to $2.2 billion, respectively.

- Nuclear: $775 million to $1,235 million (59% increase)
- Fossil Fuel: $531 million in 2002 and 2007 (0% increase)
- Renewable: $248 million to $305 million (23% increase)[2]
  - Solar: increased from $126 million to $203 million (60% increase)

---

[2] Funding for hydrogen increased 154%; however, this fuel type was not allocated to electricity since it is used primarily as an alternative fuel for transportation.

o   Geothermal: decreased from $36 million to $6 million (84% decrease)

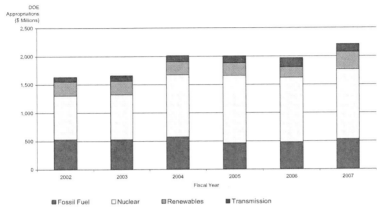

Source: GAO analysis of data provided by DOE.

Figure 3. DOE Funding for Electricity-Related R&D Increased 35% from FY2002 to FY2007 (in 2007 dollars)

Table 2. DOE Electricity-Related Funding Varied Widely across Fuels in FY2007

Fuel Sources and Transmission	Types of Fuels	Total Energy Subsidies ($ Millions)[a]	Percent Used for Electricity	Net Electricity Subsidies ($ Millions)	Electricity Generation - Megawatt-Hours
Fossil	Coal	$572.8	91.9%	$526.5	1,955.7
	Oil	3.6	2.3%	0.1	98.7
	Natural Gas	16.1	25.4%	4.1	643.6
Nuclear	Nuclear	1,235.3	100.0%	1,235.3	780.3
Renewable	Hydrogen	246.1	0.0%	0.0	0.0
	Biomass	253.9	13.3%	33.9	23.3
	Solar	202.6	100.0%	202.6	0.6
	Wind	62.7	100.0%	62.7	15.9
	Geothermal	6.4	91.0%	5.8	14.6
	Hydropower	0.0	98.7%	0.0	269.9
Transmission	All Above	137.0	100.0%	137.0	--
Total		$2,736.6		$2,208.0	

Sources: DOE Fiscal Year 2007 Operating Plan and EIA Annual Energy Review 2006.

[a] Program management allocated on a pro rata basis to individual fuel types.

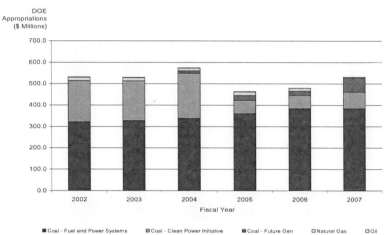

Source: GAO analysis of data provided by DOE.

Figure 4. DOE Funding for Electricity-Related Fossil Fuel R&D Varied Slightly from FY2002 to FY2007 (2007 dollars)

Table 3. DOE Funding for Electricity-Related Fossil Fuels R&D Programs in FY2007

Fuel Type	Program	Description	FY2007 ($ Millions)
Coal	Fuels and Power Systems	Provides research to reduce coal power plant emissions and improve efficiency to reduce carbon emissions.	$385.0
	Clean Coal Power Initiative	Enables and accelerates deployment of advanced technologies to ensure that the United States has clean, reliable, and affordable electricity.	74.7
	FutureGen	Focuses on the technical capability of coproducing electricity and hydrogen with near-zero atmospheric emissions.	66.8
Natural Gas	Natural Gas Technologies	Develop technologies to locate and produce gas from nonconventional reservoirs	4.1
Oil	Oil Technologies	Develop technologies to resolve the environmental, supply, and reliability constraints of producing oil resources.	0.1
Total Fossil Fuel			$530.7

Source: GAO analysis of data provided by DOE.

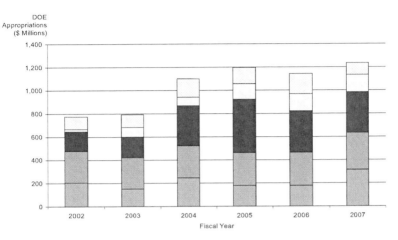

Source: GAO analysis of data provided by DOE.

Figure 5. DOE Funding for Electricity-Related Nuclear R&D Increased from FY2002 to FY2007 (2007 dollars)

Table 4. DOE Funding for Electricity-Related Nuclear R&D Programs in FY2007

Fuel Type	Program	Description	FY2007 ($ Millions)
Nuclear Energy	Environmental Cleanup	Complete the safe clean up of the environmental legacy of five decades of nuclear energy research.	$349.7
	Fusion Energy Research	National research effort to advance the knowledge base needed for an economic and environmentally attractive fusion energy source.	319.0
	Advanced Fuel Cycle Initiative	Focuses on the reduction of nuclear fuel waste needing geologic disposal and the recovery of spent nuclear fuel energy.	313.6
	Nuclear Power 2010	Joint government/industry effort to identify sites for new nuclear power plants, develop advanced standardized nuclear plant designs, and evaluate the business case for building new nuclear power plants.	150.4
	Other Nuclear Programs	Includes Generation IV Nuclear Energy Systems Initiative and the Nuclear Hydrogen Initiative.	102.7
Total Nuclear			$1,235.3

Source: GAO analysis of data provided by DOE.

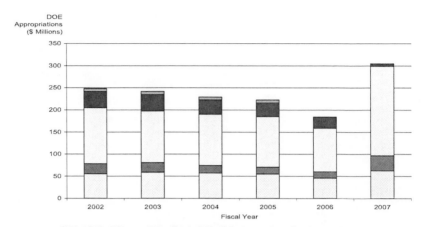

Source: GAO analysis of data provided by DOE.

Figure 6. DOE Funding for Electricity-Related Renewable R&D Decreased until FY2007 (2007 dollars)

Table 5. DOE Funding for Electricity-Related Renewable R&D Programs in FY2007

Fuel Type	Program	Description	FY2007 ($ Millions)
Renewable	Solar	Develop and accelerate the widespread commercialization of clean solar energy technologies.	$202.6
	Wind	Improve wind energy technology and address barriers to the use of wind energy.	62.7
	Biomass	Develop technologies for the successful deployment of refineries utilizing biomass resources (plant-derived material).	33.9
	Geothermal	Develop the economic production of geothermal systems and conduct field verification tests of new technology.	5.8
	Hydropower	Develop advanced technology to enhance environmental performance and operational efficiency.	0.0
Total Renewable			$305.0

Source: GAO analysis of data provided by DOE.

Tax Expenditures

Tax Expenditures are Large and Growing Support Provided to Electricity Production

We estimate electricity-related tax expenditures totaled $18.2 billion from FY2002 to FY2007 (2007 dollars).[3]

- $13.7 billion for fossil fuels
- $2.8 billion for renewables
- $1.7 billion for transmission
- None assigned to nuclear

Electricity-related tax expenditures increased from $2.2 billion to $4.1 billion (2007 dollars) from FY2002 to FY2007.

- Fossil fuels: $1.9 billion to $2.7 billion (43% increase)
- Renewables: $238 million to $790 million (232% increase)

Many tax expenditures applied to multiple fuels

- We made assignments to fuels based, in part, on EIA data.

Many electricity-related tax expenditures created since 2005, others extended or expanded.

Table 6. Several Key Tax Expenditures Apply to Multiple Fuels

Tax expenditure	Eligible fuels
New technology credit (credit for renewable electricity production and credit for renewable energy investment)[4]	Wind, biomass, poultry waste, geothermal, solar, small irrigation power, municipal solid waste, hydropower, refined coal, and Indian coal, plus fuel cells and microturbines.

---

[3] Summing tax expenditures does not take into account interactions between individual provisions.

[4] The new technology credit includes both a tax credit for production of electricity from renewable fuels and a tax credit for business investment in renewable fuel energy equipment. Currently, 10 renewable fuels and 2 renewable fuel technologies are eligible for the credit. We were unable to identify sufficient criteria to allocate revenue loss estimates for the credit to the specific fuels and technologies. Three fuels—wind, geothermal, and solar energy—likely receive the bulk of the credit.

Table 6. (Continued)

Tax expenditure	Eligible fuels
Alternative fuel production credit	Synthetic fuels produced from coal and gas produced from biomass.
Clean Renewable Energy Bond credit (CREBs)	Projects may include wind facilities, closed and open loop biomass facilities, geothermal or solar facilities, small irrigation power facilities, landfill gas facilities, trash combustion facilities, refined coal production facilities, and certain hydropower facilities.

Dollars in millions (in constant 2007 dollars)

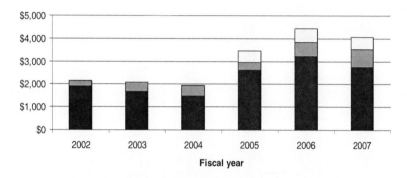

■ Fossil fuels ▨ Renewables ▢ Electricity production unassigned

Source: GAO analysis of tax expenditure data in OMB budget reports for fiscal years 2004-2008.

Note: Summing tax expenditure estimates does not take into account interactions between individual provisions.

Figure 7. Electricity-Related Tax Expenditures Increased from $2.2 billion to $4.1 Billion from FY2002 to FY2007 (2007 dollars)

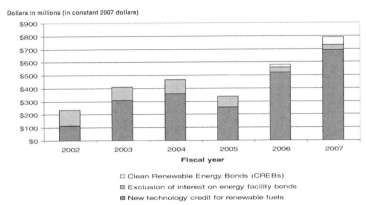

Dollars in millions (in constant 2007 dollars)

☐ Clean Renewable Energy Bonds (CREBs)
▨ Exclusion of interest on energy facility bonds
▩ New technology credit for renewable fuels

Source: GAO analysis of tax expenditure data in OMB budget reports for fiscal years 2004-2008.

Note: Summing tax expenditure estimates does not take into account interactions between individual provisions.

Figure 8. Electricity-related Tax Expenditures for Renewable Fuels Grew from $238 million to $790 million from FY2002 to FY2007 (2007 dollars)

Table 7. Most CREBs Set to Finance Solar and Wind Projects

Borrowers and Projects Receiving Initial CREB Volume Cap Allocations

Borrower	Type of project						
	Solar	Wind	Landfill gas	Open-loop biomass	Hydropower	Refined coal production	Total
Governmental	401	99	23	1	8	0	532
Cooperative	33	13	13	12	6	1	78
Total	434	112	36	13	14	1	610

Source: Internal Revenue Service.

Note: The national limit on CREBs is $1.2 billion of which a maximum of $750 million can be granted to governmental bodies.

Clean Renewable Energy Bonds (CREBs) Provide Financing for Renewable Energy Projects

The Energy Policy Act of 2005 (Pub. L. No. 109-58) authorized Treasury to allocate an $800 million volume cap in tax credit bonds to fund projects that can generate clean renewable energy.

Electric cooperatives and state and local governmental bodies have the ability to issue CREBs.

In November 2006, IRS reported that 610 projects for state and local governmental and electrical cooperative borrowers will receive authority to issue tax credit bonds under the CREBs program.

The Tax Relief and Health Care Act of 2006 (Pub. L. No. 109-432) increased the volume cap for CREBs to $1.2 billion and extended the program until December 31, 2008.

Tax credit bonds provide a greater subsidy than state and local government tax-exempt (municipal) bonds because the issuer does not pay interest.

Dollars in millions (in constant 2007 dollars)

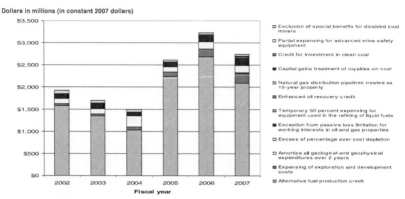

Source: GAO analysis of tax expenditure data in OMB budget reports for fiscal years 2004-2008.

Note: Summing tax expenditure estimates does not take into account interactions between individual provisions.

Figure 9. Electricity-related Tax Expenditures for Fossil Fuels Grew from $1.9 billion to over $2.7 billion from FY2002 to FY2007 (2007 dollars)

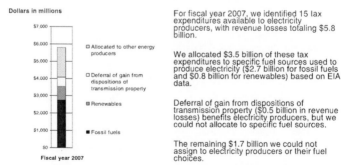

For fiscal year 2007, we identified 15 tax expenditures available to electricity producers, with revenue losses totaling $5.8 billion.

We allocated $3.5 billion of these tax expenditures to specific fuel sources used to produce electricity ($2.7 billion for fossil fuels and $0.8 billion for renewables) based on EIA data.

Deferral of gain from dispositions of transmission property ($0.5 billion in revenue losses) benefits electricity producers, but we could not allocate to specific fuel sources.

The remaining $1.7 billion we could not assign to electricity producers or their fuel choices.

Source: GAO analysis of tax expenditure data in OMB budget reports for fiscal years 2004-2008.

Note: Summing tax expenditure estimates does not take into account interactions between individual provisions.

Figure 10. Tax Expenditures for Fuels Used for Electricity Production, FY2007

Table 8. FY2007 Electricity-Related Tax Expenditure Estimates

Tax expenditure related to electricity production in fiscal year 2007	Total tax expenditure estimate	Assigned to electricity
Credit for holding clean renewable energy bonds (CREBs)	$60	$60
Credit for investment in clean coal (power generation) facilities	30	27
Credit for alternative fuel production	2,370	2,095
Exclusion of interest on energy facility bonds	40	40
New technology credit	690	690
Amortize all geological and geophysical expenditures over 2 years	60	16
Exception from passive loss limitation for working interests in oil and gas properties	30	6
Excess of percentage over cost depletion, fuels	790	160
Expensing of exploration and development costs, fuels	860	224
Natural gas distribution pipelines treated as 15-year property	50	15
Partial expensing for advanced mine safety equipment	10	9
Exclusion of special benefits for disabled coal miners	50	44
Capital gains treatment of royalties on coal	170	150
Temporary 50% expensing for equipment used in the refining of liquid fuels	30	1
Deferral of gain from dispositions of transmission property to implement Federal Energy Regulatory Commission (FERC) restructuring policy	530	530
Sum of tax expenditure revenue loss estimates	$5,770	$4,067

Source: GAO analysis of tax expenditure data in OMB budget report for fiscal year 2008.

Note: Summing tax expenditure estimates does not take into account interactions between individual provisions.

Table 9. FY2007 Electricity-Related Tax Expenditure Estimates by Fuel Source

Tax expenditure related to electricity production in fiscal year 2007	Assigned to electricity			
	Fossil fuel	Renewables	Not assigned	Estimate sum
Credit for holding clean renewable energy bonds (CREBs)	$0	$60	$0	$60
Credit for investment in clean coal (power generation) facilities	27	0	0	27
Credit for alternative fuel production	2,095	0	0	2,095
Exclusion of interest on energy facility bonds	0	40	0	40
New technology credit	0	690	0	690

Table 9. (Continued)

Tax expenditure related to electricity production in fiscal year 2007	Assigned to electricity			
	Fossil fuel	Renewables	Not assigned	Estimate sum
Amortize all geological and geophysical expenditures over 2 years	16	0	0	16
Exception from passive loss limitation for working interests in oil and gas properties	6	0	0	6
Excess of percentage over cost depletion, fuels	160	0	0	160
Expensing of exploration and development costs, fuels	224	0	0	224
Natural gas distribution pipelines treated as 15-year property	15	0	0	15
Partial expensing for advanced mine safety equipment	9	0	0	9
Exclusion of special benefits for disabled coal miners	44	0	0	44
Capital gains treatment of royalties on coal	150	0	0	150
Temporary 50% expensing for equipment used in the refining of liquid fuels	1	0	0	1
Deferral of gain from dispositions of transmission property to implement FERC restructuring policy	0	0	530	530
Sum of tax expenditure revenue loss estimates	$2,747	$790	$530	$4,067

Source: GAO analysis of tax expenditure data in OMB budget report for fiscal year 2008.

Note: Summing tax expenditure estimates does not take into account interactions between individual provisions.

GAO Recommended Examining Tax Expenditures alongside Related Spending and Reevaluating the Energy R&D Funding Mix

GAO has recommended that tax expenditures be considered alongside related spending programs in performance reviews and recommended developing a framework for evaluating tax expenditures.[5]

Review of major programs and policies, including tax expenditures, can help establish their relevance to today's needs, and direct scarce resources to the most effective tools to deliver federal support.

GAO has suggested that Congress consider focusing more of the R&D funding mix on advanced energy technologies.[6]

---

[5] GAO, Government Performance and Accountability: Tax Expenditures Represent a Substantial Federal Commitment and Need to Be Reexamined, GAO-05-690 (Washington, D.C.: Sept. 23, 2005).

For biofuels,[7] GAO recommended that DOE

- Develop a strategic approach to coordinate a range of production and distribution programs and policies
- Collaborate with Treasury in evaluating the extent to which biofuel-related tax expenditures are achieving their goals

A number of electricity-related tax expenditures enacted or expanded in 2005 are set to expire in coming years. Congressional review prior to expiration could offer an opportunity to examine the results and consider which to keep, modify, or eliminate.

- Examine alongside related program funding.
- Examine coordination between DOE and Treasury.

Other Ways the Federal Government May Subsidize Electricity

GAO Identified Specific Areas that Would Require Additional Work to Evaluate

1. Federal government provides some federal electricity producers with access to low-cost financing
2. USDA Rural Development loans money to some electricity producers and sellers at low interest rates
3. New program at DOE could expand loan guarantees for renewables and nuclear
4. USDA electricity-related programs support electricity
5. DOE's Tribal Energy Activities Program and Renewable Energy Production Incentives Program encourage development of renewable energy sources
6. Price-Anderson Act limits nuclear operator liability

---

[6] GAO, Department of Energy: Key Challenges Remain for Developing and Deploying Advanced Energy Technologies to Meet Future Needs, GAO-07-106 (Washington, D.C.: Dec. 20, 2006).

[7] GAO, Biofuels: DOE Lacks a Strategic Approach to Coordinate Increasing Production with Infrastructure Development and Vehicle Needs, GAO-07-713 (Washington, D.C.: June 8, 2007).

7. Decontamination and decommissioning of nuclear fuel manufacturing facilities may result in federal costs
8. Construction and operation of commercial nuclear reactor waste storage may result in federal costs

Federal Government Provides Low-Cost Financing to Federal Electricity Producers

Federal entities have access to low-cost financing.

- Power marketing administrations (PMAs) other than the Bonneville Power Administration (BPA) finance capital expenditures through federally appropriated debt repaid at various terms.
- BPA is responsible for repaying previously appropriated debt, federal borrowing, and nonfederal debt related to several capital expenditures.
  - Columbia River Power System
  - Corps of Engineers fish-related investment
  - BPA transmission investments made prior to 1978
  - Corps of Engineers and Bureau of Reclamation hydroelectric improvements
- The Tennessee Valley Authority finances capital expenditures through privately issued bonds that are highly rated due to perceived federal guarantee (despite notation on bonds).

Low cost of borrowing may amount to a subsidy.

- Critics have noted these rates, terms, and conditions may be preferential compared to market rates, terms, and conditions.

Methodologies to measure subsidies can produce a range of results. More work could be done:

- Detailed comparison of rates, terms and conditions
- Identification of appropriate comparison group

PMA and BPA Borrowing May Constitute a Subsidy
PMAs and BPA use appropriated debt.

- PMAs other than BPA receive appropriations for capital expenditures (called appropriated debt).
- Western Area Power Administration (WAPA), Southeastern Power Administration (SEPA), and Southwestern Power Administration (SWPA) use appropriated debt.
- BPA repays previously appropriated debt and uses other federal borrowing.
  - o In FY1997, BPA's appropriated debt was restructured from $6.85 billion, with an average interest rate of 3.5 percent, to $4.1 billion, with an interest rate of 7.1 percent.
  - o BPA estimated the present value of the principal after restructuring increased by $100 million.
  - o BPA also uses direct federal borrowing and acquires some capital assets via private sector lease.

Appropriated debt must be repaid with interest and outstanding appropriated debt may constitute a subsidy.

- A net financing cost can exist if PMA interest rates are below Treasury rates.
- As of September 30, 2006, weighted average interest rates for outstanding appropriated debt are:
- SEPA 4.7%
- SWPA 3.2%
- WAPA 5.5%
- BPA 6.7%

TVA's Implicit Federal Guarantees on Borrowed Funds May Reduce Borrowing Costs and Amount to a Subsidy
TVA borrows from private debt markets.

- TVA is authorized to issue bonds and notes in private markets.
- Authority to issue bonds and notes is set by Congress and currently cannot exceed $30 billion outstanding at any given time.

TVA bonds are highly rated due, in part, to perceived federal backing.

- Debt rating services (Standard and Poor's, Moody's, Fitch) give TVA credit their highest ratings.
- According to Standard and Poor's, TVA's rating "reflects the U.S. government's implicit support of TVA due to its status as a wholly owned government corporation, despite the lack of a binding legal obligation, as well as the authority's underlying business and financial risk."

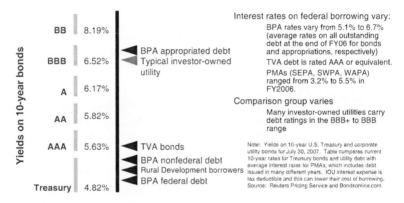

Figure 11. Federal Debt Generally Pays Favorable Rates Relative to Private Debt Ratings

USDA Rural Development Lends Money to Some Electricity Producers and Sellers at Low Interest Rates

USDA Rural Development provides loans and loan guarantees to rural electric cooperatives at low rates.

- Cooperatives generally serve areas that are historically rural, but may now include some portions of highly populated metropolitan areas.

Rural Development loans may provide a subsidy.

- Rural Development interest rates may be lower than market rates.
- Rural Development loan defaults could end up costing the federal government money.

Rural Development provides an estimate of the subsidy associated with its loans.

- GAO has not done recent work to review Rural Development estimates or otherwise evaluate potential subsidies.

More work is needed to develop robust estimates of potential subsidies.

- Detailed comparison of rates, terms, and conditions of Rural Development loans to those available to comparable entities.
- Identification of appropriate comparable entities.

USDA Rural Development

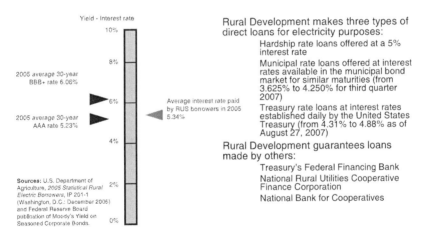

Rural Development makes three types of direct loans for electricity purposes:
Hardship rate loans offered at a 5% interest rate
Municipal rate loans offered at interest rates available in the municipal bond market for similar maturities (from 3.625% to 4.250% for third quarter 2007)
Treasury rate loans at interest rates established daily by the United States Treasury (from 4.31% to 4.88% as of August 27, 2007)
Rural Development guarantees loans made by others:
Treasury's Federal Financing Bank
National Rural Utilities Cooperative Finance Corporation
National Bank for Cooperatives

Figure 12. Rural Development Provides Loans Directly and Guarantees Loans Made by Others

Estimated Subsidy Costs of Loans and Loan Guarantees
Authorized amounts of Rural Development electricity loan and loan guarantee totaled $21.9 billion from FY2002 to FY2006.

- Loan disbursements from these authorized funds total $14.9 billion, according to the most recent USDA estimates.
- Current estimate of the subsidy cost for the disbursed portion of these loan and loan guarantees are $2.4 million.

Other Ways the Federal Government May Subsidize Electricity

New Program at DOE Could Expand Loan Guarantees for Renewables and Nuclear

Incentives for Innovative Technologies Loan Guarantee Program

- Authorized by the 2005 Energy Policy Act.

DOE has yet to fund projects under this program.

- Potentially eligible projects include renewable energy systems and advanced nuclear energy facilities.
- For fiscal year 2007, Congress provided DOE with authority to issue guarantees for up to $4 billion in loans.
- For fiscal year 2008, DOE requested $9 billion in loan guarantee authority.

GAO is required to annually review the status of this program.

Other USDA Programs Support Electricity

The Farm Security and Rural Investment Act of 2002 added or augmented several provisions to support renewable energy, such as wind power's growth, including

- Conservation Reserve Program
- Business and Industry Direct Loan and Loan Guarantee Program
- Value-Added Agriculture Product Market Development Grants
- Energy Audit and Renewable Energy Development Program
- Renewable Energy Systems and Energy Efficiency Improvements

We reported in September 2004[8] that many USDA stakeholders considered the Renewable Energy Program the key USDA program for promoting renewable energy sources on farms, ranches, or other rural lands.

---

[8] GAO, Renewable Energy: Wind Power's Contribution to Electric Power Generation and Impact on Farms and Rural Communities, GAO-04-756 (Washington, D.C.: Sept. 3, 2004).

USDA Renewable Energy Program

Table 10. Dollar Amounts of Grants Offered and Loans Guaranteed, FY2003 to FY2006

Renewable technology	Fiscal year				FY02-06 total
	2003	2004	2005	2006	
Grant program					
Wind	$7,388,903	$7,886,830	$12,533,783	$5,417,525	$33,277,041
Biomass-anaerobic digester	7,446,530	9,508,946	5,018,017	2,880,957	24,854,450
Biomass-bioenergy	2,529,005	3,133,844	2,118,391	6,993,218	14,774,458
Energy efficiency	1,504,252	1,815,262	1,610,429	4,512,936	9,442,879
Hybrid systems	2,112,977	126,992	199,863	81,404	2,521,236
Solar	725,566	54,822	661,855	782,396	2,224,639
Geothermal	0	285,353	94,930	540,999	921,282
Grant program total	$21,707,233	$22,812,049	$22,237,268	$21,209,435	$87,965,985
Loan guarantee program					
Wind				$279,111	$279,111
Biomass-anaerobic digester				1,065,850	$1,065,850
Biomass-bioenergy			10,100,000	22,212,821	32,312,821
Energy efficiency				601,080	$601,080
Loan guarantee program total			$10,100,000	$24,158,862	$34,258,862

Source: USDA.

Other Ways the Federal Government May Subsidize Electricity

DOE's Tribal Energy Activities Program and Renewable Energy Production Incentives Program Encourage Development of Renewable Energy Sources

DOE's Tribal Energy Activities Program helps assess Native American energy needs and provides technical and financial assistance for energy efficiency and renewable energy project developments.

- From FY2002 to FY2007, this program received $28.7 million in funding (in 2007 dollars).

DOE's Renewable Energy Production Initiatives Program provides financial incentive payments for renewable energy electricity produced and sold by qualified renewable energy generation facilities.

- Qualifying facilities are eligible for annual incentive payments of 1.5 cents per kilowatt-hour (1993 dollars and indexed for inflation) for the first 10-year period of their operation. Funds are subject to the availability of annual appropriations.
- From fiscal years 2002 to 2007, this program received $29.1 million in funding (in 2007 dollars).

GAO has not evaluated the effectiveness of these programs.

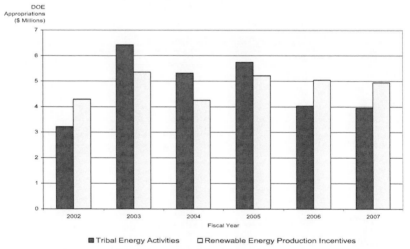

Source: GAO analysis of data provided by DOE and EIA.

Figure 13. DOE Funding for Tribal Energy Activities and Renewable Energy Production Incentives Similar from FY2002 to FY2007 (in 2007 dollars)

Price-Anderson Act Limits Nuclear Operator Liability

Price-Anderson Act, as amended, sets liability limits and establishes insurance requirements.

- Establishes requirement for operators to purchase primary insurance. The amount is currently set at $300 million per plant.

- Creates a secondary retrospective insurance pool of about $10 billion (in 2006).
- Congress will determine plans and sources of funds, including possible industry sources, if an accident occurs that results in damages exceeding this limit.

Price-Anderson Act may constitute a subsidy.

- Limits the insurance needs and premium costs of the industry.

No credible quantification of the value is available.
Estimating the value will require among other things

- Estimate of the probability of an extraordinary nuclear occurrence for each plant, and
- Estimate of the extent of potential offsite economic damages.

Decontamination and Decommissioning of Nuclear Fuel Manufacturing Facilities May Result in Federal Costs
Federal government has had a role in uranium enrichment.

- For several decades, the federal government was responsible for nuclear fuel production (uranium enrichment) in the United States.
- Uranium Enrichment Decontamination and Decommissioning Fund established under Energy Policy Act of 1992. Unless reauthorized by Congress, contributions to the Fund will end in 2007.

May constitute a subsidy

- If the Fund is insufficient and the federal government pays for costs attributable to commercial nuclear operations, a potential subsidy exists.

Little is known about the value of this potential subsidy.

- GAO estimated costs could exceed fund by $100 million to $4.2 billion[9] (in 2007 dollars).

Estimating the value will require among things

- Cost and schedule to complete decontamination and decommissioning of facilities.
- Potential congressional actions if the fund is insufficient. Action may depend on DOE report that will be available by the end of 2007.

Construction and Operation of a Geologic Repository for Disposal of Radioactive Waste May Result in Federal Costs

The federal government is to build and operate a facility to permanently dispose of waste.

- Nuclear Waste Policy Act of 1982 directs DOE to take title to and dispose of nuclear waste by 1998.
- DOE efforts to develop a permanent repository are required by statute to be solely focused on a yet-to-be-built repository at Yucca Mountain, Nevada. Most recent estimate is that facility will not be ready before 2017.
- Nuclear Waste Fund fees collected on nuclear power generation are set to fully recover estimated cost due to nuclear power of building and operating a geologic repository.

There may be an implicit subsidy in the program because, under the Act, the federal government has potentially assumed risks of cost over runs and schedule delays for the repository.

- A shortfall in the fund could become a potential government liability if fees are not adjusted.

---

[9] GAO, Uranium Enrichment: Decontamination and Decommissioning Fund Is Insufficient to Cover Cleanup Costs, GAO-04-692 (Washington, D.C.: July 2, 2004).

- Government liabilities to nuclear power companies approaching $7 billion are for failing to comply with the statutory requirement that DOE begin disposing of waste by 1998.

Additional work required to evaluate trust fund balances and potential subsidy, if any.

Selected GAO Products Related to Electricity Subsidies

General

National Energy Policy: Inventory of Major Federal Energy Programs and Status of Policy Recommendations. GAO-05-379. Washington, D.C.: June 10, 2005.

Federal Research and Development

Department of Energy: Key Challenges Remain for Developing and Deploying Advanced Energy Technologies to Meet Future Needs. GAO-07-106. Washington, D.C.: December 20, 2006.
Federal Research: Changes in Electricity-Related R&D Funding. GAO/RCED-96-203. Washington, D.C.: August 16, 1996.

Tax Expenditures

Biofuels: DOE Lacks a Strategic Approach to Coordinate Increasing Production with Infrastructure Development and Vehicle Needs. GAO-07-713. June 8, 2007.
Government Performance and Accountability: Tax Expenditures Represent a Substantial Federal Commitment and Need to Be Reexamined. GAO-05-690. September 23, 2005.

Renewable Energy

Renewable Energy: Wind Power's Contribution to Electric Power Generation and Impact on Farms and Rural Communities. GAO-04-756. Washington, D.C.: September 3, 2004.

Rural Utilities Service

Rural Utilities Service: Opportunities to Better Target Assistance to Rural Areas and Avoid Unnecessary Financial Risk. GAO-04-647. Washington, D.C.: June 18, 2004.
Rural Development: Financial Condition of the Rural Utilities Service's Loan Portfolio. GAO/RCED-97-82. April 11, 1997.

Power Marketing Administration/Bonneville Power Administration/ Tennessee Valley Authority

Bonneville Power Administration: Better Management of BPA's Obligation to Provide Power Is Needed to Control Future Costs. GAO-04-694. Washington, D.C.: July 9, 2004.

Tennessee Valley Authority: Bond Ratings Based on Ties to the Federal Government and Other Nonfinancial Factors. GAO-01-540. Washington, D.C.: April 30, 2001.

Federal Electricity Activities: The Federal Government's Net Cost and Potential for Future Losses Volume 1. GAO/AIMD-97-110. Washington, D.C.: September 19, 1997.

Federal Electricity Activities: Appendixes to The Federal Government's Net Cost and Potential for Future Losses Volume 2. GAO/AIMD-97-110A. Washington, D.C.: September 19, 1997.

Power Marketing Administrations: Cost Recovery, Financing, and Comparison to Nonfederal Utilities. GAO/AIMD-96-145. Washington, D.C.: September 19, 1996.

Federal Loan Guarantee Programs

The Department of Energy: Key Steps Needed to Help Ensure the Success of the New Loan Guarantee Program for Innovative Technologies by Better Managing Its Financial Risk. GAO-07-339R. Washington, D.C.: February 28, 2007.

Nuclear Issues

Uranium Enrichment: Decontamination and Decommissioning Fund Is Insufficient to Cover Cleanup Costs. GAO-04-692. Washington, D.C.: July 2, 2004.

REFERENCES

[1] All dollar amounts for R&D funding and tax expenditures discussed in this report are inflation adjusted to 2007 dollars. Of the $11.5 billion amount, we could assign $10.7 billion to fuel types. The remaining unassigned portion of R&D funding was related to efforts to improve the transmission of electricity. In nominal dollars, we estimate that DOE's appropriations for electricity-related R&D totaled $10.8 billion from fiscal year 2002 through fiscal year 2007.

[2] Summing tax expenditure estimates provides a gauge of general magnitude but does not take into account interactions between individual provisions. Of the $18.2 billion amount, we could assign $16.5 billion to fuel types. We could not assign one electricity-related tax expenditure, deferral of gain from dispositions of transmission property, to a fuel type. This tax expenditure totaled $1.7 billion during the period of our analysis. All tax expenditure estimates are based on projections using prior year data; whereas historical data are available for federal receipts and outlays, the last available values for tax expenditures remain estimates.

[3] The tax credit for alternative fuel is scheduled to expire at the end of calendar year 2007. If this tax credit expires, the total tax expenditures for fossil fuels used for electricity production would fall significantly.

[4] The PMAs are BPA, Southeastern Power Administration, Southwestern Power Administration, and Western Area Power Administration.

[5] The Rural Utilities Service, an agency of USDA, will be referred to in this report as Rural Development.

INDEX